If I Were a Dolphin

By Meg Gaertner

level
2
little blue
readers

www.littlebluehousebooks.com

Copyright © 2021 by Little Blue House, Mendota Heights, MN 55120. All rights reserved. No part of this book may be reproduced or utilized in any form or by any means without written permission from the publisher.

Little Blue House is distributed by North Star Editions:
sales@northstareditions.com | 888-417-0195

Produced for Little Blue House by Red Line Editorial.

Photographs ©: iStockphoto, cover, 4, 6–7, 10, 13 (top), 13 (bottom), 14–15, 17 (top), 17 (bottom), 18, 21 (top), 21 (bottom), 22–23, 24 (top left), 24 (top right), 24 (bottom left), 24 (bottom right); Shutterstock Images, 9

Library of Congress Control Number: 2020913850

ISBN
978-1-64619-303-5 (hardcover)
978-1-64619-321-9 (paperback)
978-1-64619-357-8 (ebook pdf)
978-1-64619-339-4 (hosted ebook)

Printed in the United States of America
Mankato, MN
012021

About the Author

Meg Gaertner enjoys reading, writing, dancing, and being outside. She loves learning about how smart dolphins are. She lives in Minnesota.

Table of Contents

If I Were a Dolphin

I would live in the water.

But I would come up

for air.

I would have a strong tail.
My tail would move up
and down.

I would swim to the water's surface, and I would breathe air.

air

water

Body and Behavior

I would have gray skin.

My back would be darker than my front.

I would have many teeth.

I would eat fish and squid.

I would have a
curved mouth.
I would look like
I was smiling.

mouth

I would swim quickly, and I would jump out of the water.

pod

Life in a Pod

I would swim in a pod.

A pod is a group

of dolphins.

I would hunt and play with other dolphins. We would keep one another safe from sharks.

21

I would have one baby.
My baby would be dark in color.

Glossary

pod

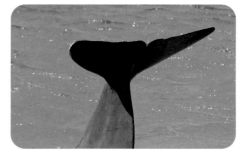

tail

shark

teeth

Index